CAN YOU
ESCAPE
THE MEDIEVAL CASTLE?

weldon**owen**

weldonowen

Written by Stella Caldwell

Copyright © Weldon Owen Children's Books, 2022

All rights reserved. No part of this publication may be reproduced, distributed, or transmitted in any form or by any means, including photocopying, recording, or other electronic or mechanical methods, without the prior written permission of the publisher, except in the case of brief quotations embodied in critical reviews and certain other noncommercial uses permitted by copyright law.

Published by Weldon Owen Children's Books
An imprint of Weldon Owen International, L.P.
A subsidiary of Insight International, L.P.
PO Box 3088
San Rafael, CA 94912
www.insighteditions.com

Weldon Owen Children's Books:
Designer: Tory Gordon-Harris
Editor: Miranda Smith
Senior Production Manager: Greg Steffen
Art Director: Stuart Smith
Publisher: Sue Grabham

Insight Editions:
Publisher: Raoul Goff

A CIP catalogue record of this book is available from the British Library.

ISBN: 9781915588067

Manufactured, printed, and assembled in China.
First printing, 2022. DRM0622
26 25 24 23 22   5 4 3 2 1

Picture Credits

Cover: all Shutterstock: IgorZh; Sibrikov Valery; kan_khampanya; Andrey_Kuzmin; Marcin Perkowski; Peter Gudella; Marti Bug Catcher.

Shutterstock: Throughout: parchment: Vadim Sadovski; shield: sharpner; banner: cidepix; flag: ArtVisionStudio. Single entries: 1 cosma; 8–9 Timothy Hodgkinson; ArtMari; MaxShutter; Anita SKV; 10–11 JuliaST; Terri Butler Photography; Supawat Eurthanaboon; Sergieiev; Mumemories; 12–13 Marcin Perkowski; Jacob L Stark; LCRP; ChiccoDodiFC; Elena Zajchikova; SergeyKPI; 14–15 Dario Sabljak; Fabien Monteil; New Africa; Aleksandr Stupnikov; Jaroslav Moravcik; Victor Moussa; photomaster; 16–17 Kaspars Grinvald; Szasz-Fabian Jozsef; Boltenkoff; xpixel; lomiso; Tapui; 18–19 nasidastudio; Bon Appetit; Asmus Koefoed; cdrin; Eric Isselee; irin-k; Mironmax Studio; 20–21 dtopal; grynold; Pav-Pro Photography Ltd; Matyas Rehak; quiver; quadshock; Somchai Boonpun; Radoslaw Maciejewski; 22–23 Gary Perkin; Milkovasa; 24–25 JGA; Peyker; Medwedja; Martin Bergsma; Andrey Burmaki; Alessandro de Leo; Ron Mackenzie; charl898; Heinsdorff Jularlak; svetok30; 26–27 ermess; kubais; UWBALK; Rocksweeper; Osman Temizel; Dudarev Mikhail; Vaclav Mach; Juan Carlos Cameron; VRVIRUS; Rostislav Stefanek; 28–29 schankz; michelaubryphoto; Mehmet Cetin; Pavel Savchuk; sarkao; SCOTTCHAN; Vera Petruk; Pinkasevich; Evgeny Belenkov; optimarc; VDB Photos; 30–31 Chansom Pantip; Chansom Pantip; castigatio; antoniomas; KucherAV; Ahmet Naim; 32–33 Ewa Studio; Juris Kraulis; LuXpics; Kozlik; shoricelu; Kristina Kokhanova; Ivan Smuk; Shchus; Georgios Gkoumas; 34–35 Mzorin; Kiryl Li; 36–37 Dario Lo Presti; Nattika; Germanova Antonin; Piotr Piatrousk; Katie Stevens Photography; Serge Pyun; Anita SKV; Marina_vert; Photo_Traveller; 38–39 Zoran Milutinovich; Timo Nausch; Jan Schneckenhaus; 40–41 snowbird80; 42–43 PixelSquid3d; Mihail Guta; Aman Kumar Verma; Ajdin Kamber; Mister Dreamer; 44–45 Janek Sergeje; Andres Conema; Leigh Prather; 46–47 Andranik7; charl898; Anna Krivitskaya; 48–49 Potapov Alexander; Nattapat.J; Pheerasak Jomnuy; Sanit Fuangnakhon; xpixel; 50–51 oksana2010; Bruno Bleu; tomertu; PloyKanok; Eugen Thome; The_Molostock; Dmitr1ch; 52–53 lorsoboog; McCarthy's PhotoWorks; JirkaBursik; givaga; Elizabeth A. Cummings; Bildagentur Zoonar GmbH; Glitterstudio; 54–55 7yonov; Photoexpert; Mira Drozdowski; Manbetta; SvetaKost; Florian Teodor; Kotomka Studio; 56–57 Selma ARSLAN; 58–59 Dja65; Gwoei; Stepan Bormotov; Tarebodadesign; Vitaly Korovin; O.Schaumann; Adam Hanley; 60–61 FProductions; MaraZe; donatas1205; nnattalli; 62–63 Iuri S Design; lolloj; ToskanaINC; tartaruga 1988; Pan_Da; T.W. van Urk; Aleksandra Nadeina; Chinnapong; 64–65 Lucie Lang; NEOS1AM; fggato; Yuri Turkov; Alp Galip; 66–67 Oleksandr Lysenko; Picsfive; KucherAV.

Alamy: 46–47 great hall: Chris Howes/Wild Places Photography/Alamy Stock Photo; 64–65 bed: Ian Hubball/Alamy Stock Photo.

Tim Loughead, Precision Illustration: 28–29 jester's hat; 40–41 trapdoor; 60–61 water in basin

The Metropolitan Museum of Modern Art: 36–37 candlestick: The Cloisters Collection, gift of Dr. Louis R. Slattery, 1982; jug: The Cloisters Collection, 2014; jug: gift of Anthony and Lois Blumka, 1991.

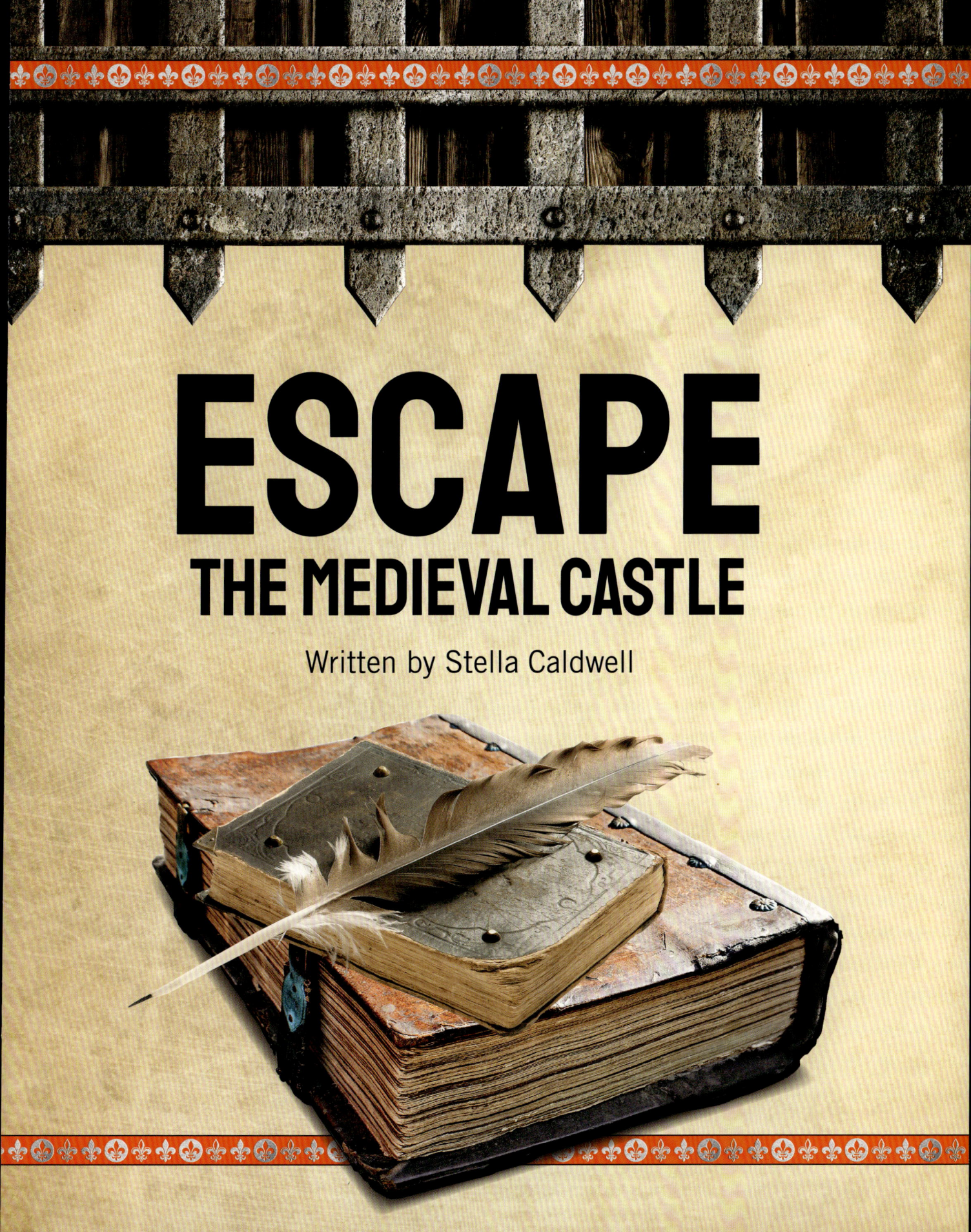

STEP BACK IN TIME TO
THE MIDDLE AGES

ARE YOU READY TO TRAVEL MORE THAN 600 YEARS BACK IN TIME, TO THE HEART OF A MEDIEVAL CASTLE?

It is 1389, and for most people in Europe, life is harsh. The majority are poor peasants who toil on the land as farmers, or who work as servants. But for the nobles born into the upper ranks of society, life is very different. The king gives them large areas of land in return for their loyalty, and many grow to be very powerful.

The nobles live in huge, impressive castles to show off their importance and to protect their realms from enemy attack. The massive stone walls can be seen from a great distance and colourful flags flap from the solid towers.

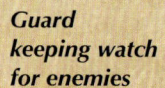

Guard keeping watch for enemies

A noble's ruby-set ring

The thick walls are designed to keep out enemies and the high towers allow the guards to spot approaching danger. Many castles are surrounded by a water-filled ditch called a moat. When the drawbridge over the moat is raised, the entrance to the castle is shut off and its people are safe.

As well as being a mighty stronghold, a castle is a magnificent home for a lord, lady and their children. Everyone else that lives there – from the knights, soldiers and guards to the priest and servants – works for or protects the noble family. The huge, hot kitchen is filled with the clamour of busy cooks, scurrying servants attend to the lord and lady's chambers and the courtyard workshops echo with the sounds of the blacksmith's hammer and the carpenter's saw. A huge fire crackles in the great hall, and on feast days, the air is filled with the sounds of loud laughter and music.

Behind a castle's great walls lie magnificent rooms, dark passageways, winding staircases and secret chambers. Here, important connections between noble families are made, dark plots are hatched and prisoners are locked away. Service and loyalty are highly valued, but danger and treachery are never far away.

IN A FEW PAGES, YOU WILL FIND YOURSELF IMPRISONED IN A MIGHTY CASTLE. DO YOU HAVE THE COURAGE TO CONTINUE?

Quiver of arrows

WILL YOU TAKE THE
ESCAPE CHALLENGE?

WELL DONE, YOU ARE DARING AND BRAVE! GET READY TO ZOOM BACK IN TIME MORE THAN 600 YEARS TO MEDIEVAL EUROPE.

Your character

You are 13 years old and live in a magnificent castle. Your father passed away two years ago and your mother, Lady Isabella, governs your home. For your sister Alianor and yourself, the castle is your home and a bustling place full of nobles, servants, craftspeople and entertainers. But it is also a mighty fortress fiercely defended by soldiers, with the threat of a siege never far away. The massive walls protect it from enemy attack, while inside is a maze of dark passageways.

How do you get imprisoned in another castle?

One chilly day in spring, you secretly take your mother's prized dagger for protection, saddle up a horse and go out in search of adventure. But as darkness falls, you get lost and stray off your family's land. Captured by guards from another castle, you are locked up in a tower. In the morning you will be sent for, and when they find out who you are, a ransom will be demanded from your family. You need to escape before that. To make matters worse, your mother's precious dagger has been taken from you!

At the beginning of the day, the guard will unlock the door to bring you food. You're determined to escape. You know that attacking a well-defended castle is difficult, so you can imagine how hard it will be for a prisoner to find a way out!

HOW DO YOU ESCAPE?

1 Start at number 1. Read the story. Follow the arrow to the next number.

AN UNEXPECTED TURN

It's not yet dawn when the door of your room suddenly creaks open for the guard to bring in your breakfast. Immediately, you are on the alert. As the guard steps into the dim room, he trips on an uneven floorboard, knocking himself out and dropping the door key. Seizing your chance, you grab the key, spring through the door and turn it in the lock.

➡ .... GO TO **97**

2 Read the following part of the story. Choose where to go next.

WHAT NOW?

97 FROM 1

You find yourself on a small landing. A narrow staircase spirals away, up and down. You know there are one or two watchmen in the turret above, and now you can hear someone coming down the stairs. He will surely raise the alarm. Should you just run for it? Or could you possibly lock him in with the other guard to gain precious time? You would need to silently unlock the door, hide just around the corner and wait for him to walk into the room.

Do you?

➤ Unlock the door, then hide and wait ..... GO TO **42**

➤ Run quickly away down the steps .... GO TO **63**

3 Read the clues carefully. They will help you to make your choices.

PLAYING RAFFLE

Raffle is a popular game played with three dice. Players place bets and take turns rolling the dice. The first player to get three of the same number is the winner.

Who is the winner?

➤ You .... GO TO **106**

➤ Guard one .... GO TO **129**

➤ Guard two .... GO TO **57**

You

Guard one

Guard two

4 Turn the wheel

When you see this symbol, consult the heraldic wheel on the front cover to find out where to go next.

CONSULT THE WHEEL
Turn to the raven symbol.

This reveals a number.

 ➤ **100**

Turn to Step 100 to continue the adventure.

If you keep your wits about you, use all the clues and make your choices wisely, you will escape the medieval castle. Turn the page if you are bold enough.

AN UNEXPECTED TURN

1 START

It's not yet dawn when the door of your room suddenly creaks open for the guard to bring in your breakfast. Immediately, you are on the alert. As the guard steps into the dim room, he trips on the uneven floor, knocking himself out and dropping the door key. Seizing your chance, you grab the key, spring through the door and turn it in the lock.

➤ .... GO TO **97**

A MAZE

2 FROM 10

Are you sure? Look closely at the words in Step 10 and think again.

Is it?

➤ An egg .... GO TO **61**

➤ A treasure chest .... GO TO **53**

LITTLE HOPE

3 FROM 100

You press yourself into the cobweb-filled shadows where it's strangely cold. As the snarling dog appears at the top of the stairs, you realise you have little chance of escaping its snapping jaws!

What do you do?

➤ Stay still and hope the dog is afraid of the ghostly shadows too .... **GO TO 95**

➤ Try to escape down the stairs .... **GO TO 123**

PIES!

4 FROM 117

You walk quickly across the courtyard into the kitchen. Inside, there's a table laden with dishes for the feast. Servants bustle around and the cook's back is turned as she cooks meat on a huge spit. Nobody is paying you any attention so you quickly shove three pies – two savoury and one sweet – into your pockets. You are starving so you reach out to grab another pie, but the cook whips round and catches you red-handed.

Do you?

➤ Mumble an apology and put the pie back .... **GO TO 13**

➤ Grab the pie anyway and try to run away .... **GO TO 33**

THE CASTLE KITCHEN

This is a hot, noisy place with huge fireplaces for spit-roasting meat, and massive pots and cauldrons for making stews and sauces. Many servants, from the head cook and undercooks to bakers, brewers and servers, help to keep the castle residents and guests fed.

DANGER!

5 FROM 21, 79

With your hand against the wall, you carefully feel your way down the steps wondering what lies at the bottom. After what feels like an age, a tiny chink of light appears . . .

➤ .... **GO TO 70**

Portcullis

THE GATEHOUSE

6 FROM 47, 61

You walk across the courtyard towards the gatehouse. The drawbridge is down, the huge portcullis is raised and the guards are engrossed in a game of dice. One of the guards looks up and demands to know your business. What should you tell them?

CONSULT THE WHEEL
Turn to the portcullis symbol.

Drawbridge over the moat to protect the castle from attack

DEFENDING THE CASTLE

The well-guarded gatehouse, or castle entrance, is the most well-defended part of the castle. When the castle is under attack, a huge grille called a portcullis can be dropped down. If attackers get past it, the defenders drop missiles or pour boiling liquid through 'murder holes' in the passageway ceiling.

A GAME

7 FROM **87, 91, 101**

The young girl cheers up when you give her the correct answer. You ask if she likes playing hide-and-seek and where the best places to hide are. 'In my father's chamber,' she instantly replies. Taking a lamp, she excitedly leads you through a maze of up-and-down passageways.

➤ .... GO TO **126**

FOOTSTEPS

8 FROM **44, 96**

You change into the servant's tunic and cap and hide your own clothes and the sword in the bottom of the chest. Then, taking the lamp, you step into the corridor. To your left is a pitch-black passage, to your right the dim glow of a room at the corridor's end. As you wonder which way to turn, the sound of someone coming out of the room leaves you no choice.

➤ .... GO TO **73**

ABANDONED TOWER

9 FROM 34

The steps are crumbling away in places and it's clear this part of the castle is rarely used. At the top, you find yourself in a windswept bell tower. It's dusk now and croaking ravens flap around menacingly. It sounds like they are trying to tell you something. Are they croaking a warning, 'Out! Out!'?

CONSULT THE WHEEL
Turn to the raven symbol.

WISE RAVEN
The raven is linked to wisdom, magic and mystery. Some believe this wise bird is able to predict the future. The raven symbol is often used in heraldry and on coats of arms, sometimes with an open beak as if 'speaking'.

RIDDLE-DI-DI

10 FROM **36**

Rattled, you run across the courtyard and crash headlong into one of the jesters from the feast! You gasp as he says, 'So that's where our costume disappeared to. *You* took it!' He looks hard at you, then suddenly laughs wildly. 'Answer this riddle correctly and I won't say a word!'

*'A wall surrounds my castle of white.
Inside you'll find a golden delight.'*

What am I?

▶ A treasure chest .... GO TO **53**

▶ An egg .... GO TO **61**

▶ A maze .... GO TO **2**

A BET

12 FROM **6**

You tell the guards you are a servant of one of the guests and ask if you can join their game. The guards ask what your bet is. You could offer one of your pies, or the last silver coin in your pocket.

LANCELOT

11 FROM **90**

Wrong! Lancelot was one of the Knights of the Round Table. Choose again.

Is it?

▶ Guinevere .... GO TO **15**

▶ Excalibur .... GO TO **36**

What do you offer?

▶ A meat pie .... GO TO **38**

▶ A silver penny .... GO TO **23**

SWORD IN THE STONE

The legend tells of how only Arthur was able to draw the sword from the stone and become king.

FOOD FOR THE FEAST
The lady of the castle is in charge of its daily running, including the care of guests. She decides the menu, choosing from what is hunted or grown on the castle's land.

A LUCKY ESCAPE

13 FROM 4

The cook glares at you in fury and goes to clip you round the ear. But just then, one of the servants calls out that something is burning. The cook rushes back to the meat, yelling, 'Get over here and turn the spit!' Should you follow her?

CONSULT THE WHEEL
Turn to the water symbol.

14 FROM 86

WOLF!

As you prepare to enter the water, the unmistakable howl of a wolf from the woods ahead fills the air. You shudder with fear.

Do you dare to cross the moat?

➤ No, you'd rather retreat than fall prey to a wolf! .... GO TO **71**

➤ Yes, you're afraid but the wolf is unlikely to harm you..... GO TO **40**

15 FROM 90

GUINEVERE

Wrong! Guinevere was King Arthur's queen. Choose again.

Is it?

➤ Lancelot .... GO TO **11**

➤ Excalibur .... GO TO **36**

Local farmers pay rent for the castle land that they farm, in goods such as wheat and rye.

IN THE STABLES

16 FROM **108**

You drop the dagger and sprint to the stables next door. Choosing a stall, you lie down behind a horse and cover yourself with straw. Soon, you see the blacksmith pacing up and down past the stalls. 'I know you're here,' he calls out. 'Come out before I find you!'

What do you do?

▶ Stay hidden and hope the blacksmith stops looking .... GO TO **31**

▶ Run away as fast as you can .... GO TO **26**

ALIANOR

17 FROM **41**

You start walking towards your sister at the top table. But just then the lord looks up and you realise it might be too risky! Should you turn around and head towards the back of the hall instead?

 **CONSULT THE WHEEL**
Turn to the throne symbol.

THE WATCHTOWER

18 FROM **30**

You creep up to the turret – thankfully, there's no second watchman. It's a relief to step outside, but as you gaze at the ground far below, you realise you're still trapped! It will be impossible to climb down the steep wall, so you turn and go down the stairs to the courtyard.

▶ .... GO TO **44**

A SORRY STATE

19 FROM 112

As you climb nearer the cage, you can see the prisoner inside is too weak to harm you – and may even be dead. You wait until the barks have faded away, then climb back. There's a distant guard to the left.

➤ .... GO TO **69**

BASIN, SPOON, KNIFE

20 FROM 81, 118

Wrong. Think carefully about it, then make your choice again.

Do you offer?

➤ Ewer, basin, napkin .... GO TO **58**

➤ Basin, knife, napkin .... GO TO **81**

21. A WAY OUT?
FROM 80

You step through the trapdoor and close it behind you. The flickering light of your candle shows steep steps that have broken away in places. You stumble, the candle slips from your hand and you find yourself in pitch darkness. You're terrified! Should you return to the bedchamber for another candle or risk feeling your way down?

Do you?

- Turn back, you might break a leg or worse .... GO TO **79**
- Keep going, you can always turn back if it becomes too difficult .... GO TO **5**

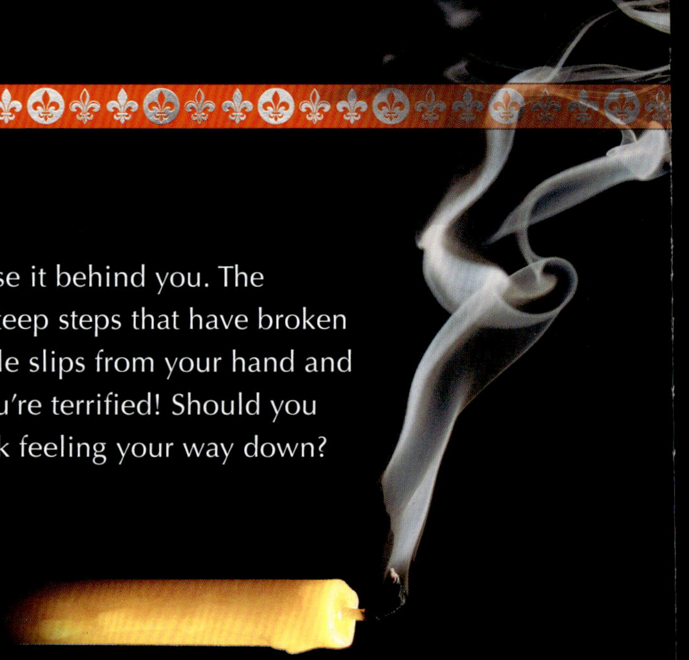

22. TRAPDOOR
FROM 67

Lying on your stomach, you lower your lamp into the deep blackness beneath the open trapdoor. With a shock, you make out a skeleton lying on the ground. Could these be the bones of a prisoner that now haunts the castle? The skeleton suddenly twitches and you leap back in horror.

▶ .... GO TO **127**

FORGOTTEN PRISONERS
If a prisoner has no value, she or he may be thrown into a pit or 'oubliette'. The word comes from the French oublier *meaning 'to forget'. But most prisoners are nobles like you, held for ransom and treated fairly.*

Prisoners are often chained to prevent escape.

A GAME OF DICE

23 FROM 12, 38

You toss the silver penny into the pot and join in the game of Raffle. When you throw a six and two fives, the first guard throws a one, a four and a five, and the second guard throws three twos.

You

Guard one

Guard two

Who is the winner?

➤ You .... GO TO **106**

➤ Guard one .... GO TO **129**

➤ Guard two .... GO TO **57**

PLAYING RAFFLE
Raffle is a popular game played with three dice. Players place bets and take turns rolling the dice. The first player to get three of the same number is the winner.

WHERE ARE YOU GOING?

24 FROM 122

You walk away from the large room, but the girl follows you to the stairs. 'Where are you going?' she asks suspiciously. Would it be wise to befriend her and try to get her help?

CONSULT THE WHEEL
Turn to the fleur de lis symbol.

Some oubliette prisoners are fed and watered but many are left to die.

INTO THE COURTYARD

25 FROM **68, 109**

You creep out into the courtyard and look around you. The sun has risen and the well-guarded gatehouse on the other side is bathed in early-morning light. In the corner, you see a well. Could this be a way out of the castle? You hurry over to the well and throw a small pebble down into the blackness. It takes several seconds before you hear a splash – it must be very deep!

➤ .... GO TO **45**

VITAL WATER SOURCE

Wells are often very deep, with the water more than 100 metres underground. The water seldom comes from a stream. Instead, it is usually groundwater, water that naturally collects underground among the rocks and soil. A reliable water source is very important, especially during a siege when it is impossible to leave the castle.

A KICK
26 FROM 16

You leap from your hiding place to run away. But the sudden movement startles the horse, and it kicks you hard in the ribs. Crying out in pain, you fall back. Just before you pass out, you see the blacksmith's furious face looming over you.

That's the end of your escape quest. You did quite well to get this far through the medieval castle!

➤ If you dare start the adventure again ... **GO TO 1**

SWORD
28 FROM 88, 104

You pull the heavy sword from the chest. But then you wonder how you'll get it out of the castle and across the moat – it will only get in the way. You put it back and select something that will be easier to carry.

Which do you choose?

➤ The ring .... **GO TO 80**

➤ The crown .... **GO TO 104**

ON THE ALERT
27 FROM 130

The guard at the gate to the inner castle sees you coming across the courtyard and starts to move towards you, probably to find out what you are doing there. Maybe you need to quickly change direction and head for the tower. What should you do?

 **CONSULT THE WHEEL**
Turn to the castle symbol.

AN ARCHER
29 FROM 113

You carry on along the battlements. If you can just reach the next tower, you'll be able to take shelter there until the coast is clear. But just as you near the door, an archer turns round and, looking straight at you, demands, 'What are you doing?'

What do you do?

➤ Run away down the tower steps .... **GO TO 54**

➤ Pretend you're running an errand ..... **GO TO 85**

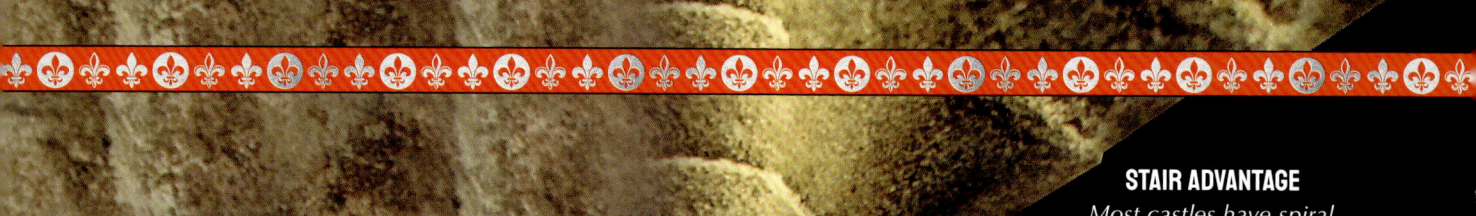

STAIR ADVANTAGE
Most castles have spiral staircases twisting in a clockwise direction. This means that an armed, right-handed person coming down the stairs has an advantage. An enemy soldier climbing up towards them has very little space to draw and swing their sword, so cannot defend themselves.

WHICH WAY?

30 FROM 42

As you catch your breath, you hear more footsteps on the stairs. You strain to listen but the sound has stopped. Is the person coming down from the watchtower above or up from the floor below? It's impossible to tell, but you need to make a decision.

What do you do?

➤ Make your way up to the watchtower .... GO TO **18**

➤ Go down the stairs to the courtyard .... GO TO **44**

TENSE MOMENTS

31 FROM 16

You hardly dare to breathe, but the blacksmith doesn't see you and eventually he leaves the stables. You wait a few minutes. Should you head for the gatehouse?

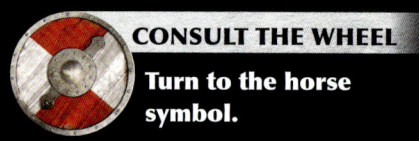
CONSULT THE WHEEL
Turn to the horse symbol.

A helmet completely covers the knight's head and gives protection against blows from swords and lances.

The breastplate covers and protects the knight's chest.

IN THE ARMOURY

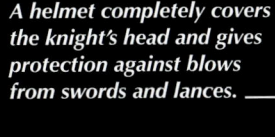
32 FROM **49**

You grab a rag and start polishing a helmet. The knight asks you to help him put on his armour as he has a tournament and he needs to practise. You often help your older brother but can you remember how to do it? If you get it wrong, the knight will be suspicious.

What order do you choose?

▶ Sabatons, greaves, breastplate, helmet .... GO TO **119**

▶ Breastplate, helmet, sabatons, greaves .... GO TO **83**

▶ Helmet, greaves, sabatons, breastplate .... GO TO **43**

Greaves, or jambeaux, are the pieces of armour that protect the legs.

The two metal sabatons protect a knight's feet.

THE RIGHT ORDER

A suit of armour is very heavy, so a knight needs help putting it on, usually from his squire. The armour needs to be strapped on in a particular order. Working up from bottom to top, the squire starts with the sabatons for the feet, and finishes with the helmet.

IN TROUBLE!

33 FROM **4**

You are caught and taken to the yard. As a punishment for stealing, you are put in the pillory to be pelted with rotten food and mud.

That's the end of your escape quest. You can't escape the pillory.

▶ If you dare to start the adventure again .... GO TO **1**

ARROW ATTACK

34 FROM 115

You climb out of the shaft and listen. There are people talking on the landing below you, so you peer out the door along the wall walk to see if the coast is clear. It is, and you walk along the battlements towards the next tower. Suddenly, an arrow whistles past your head. You break into a run and dive through the door of the tower. The steps leading down have broken away, but there is a narrow staircase leading up.

Where to now?

▶ Up the spiral staircase .... **GO TO 9**

▶ Down to the rooms below .... **GO TO 50**

LOOKING FOR LIGHT

35 FROM 77, 98

You find a small chapel next to the great hall. Inside, you can see two iron candlesticks on the altar holding unlit candles. As you take both the candles, you hear approaching footsteps. You're dressed as a servant, but would you normally be in the chapel at this early hour? You decide to hide under the altar.

 .... GO TO **109**

ON THE BATTLEMENTS
The strong outer wall of a castle is topped by the battlements, stone walls with gaps in them that run from tower to tower. The soldiers can hide from the missiles of an enemy attack while firing cannonballs and arrows through the gaps.

SECRET MESSAGE

36 FROM 90

You've remembered the name of the sword. As you slip out of the hall, you are followed by a servant who pushes something into your hand and whispers in your ear, 'This is from your sister.' You look down and see it is a scrap of parchment. You turn to ask the servant for more information but she's already disappeared.

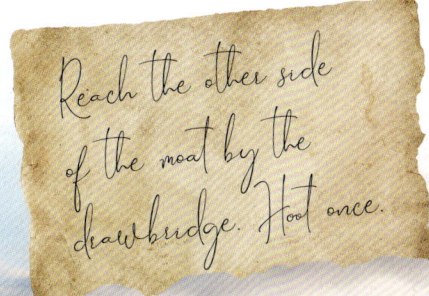

Reach the other side of the moat by the drawbridge. Hoot once.

 .... GO TO **10**

Weapons for defence
As well as firing cannonballs and arrows, soldiers shoot bolts from crossbows.

MURKY MOAT

The second you start swimming, the dagger slips from your hand and sinks. After diving down through the murky waters three times, you manage to retrieve it from the bottom of the moat. Then you climb out again. Should you throw the dagger across the moat instead?

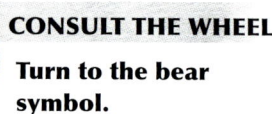 **CONSULT THE WHEEL** Turn to the bear symbol.

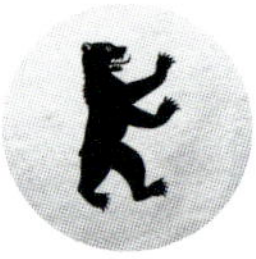

SUSPICIOUS MOVE

You reach into your pocket and bring out one of the pies. 'That's not a proper bet!' laughs one of the guards. So you find a silver coin in your pocket and add it to the pile.

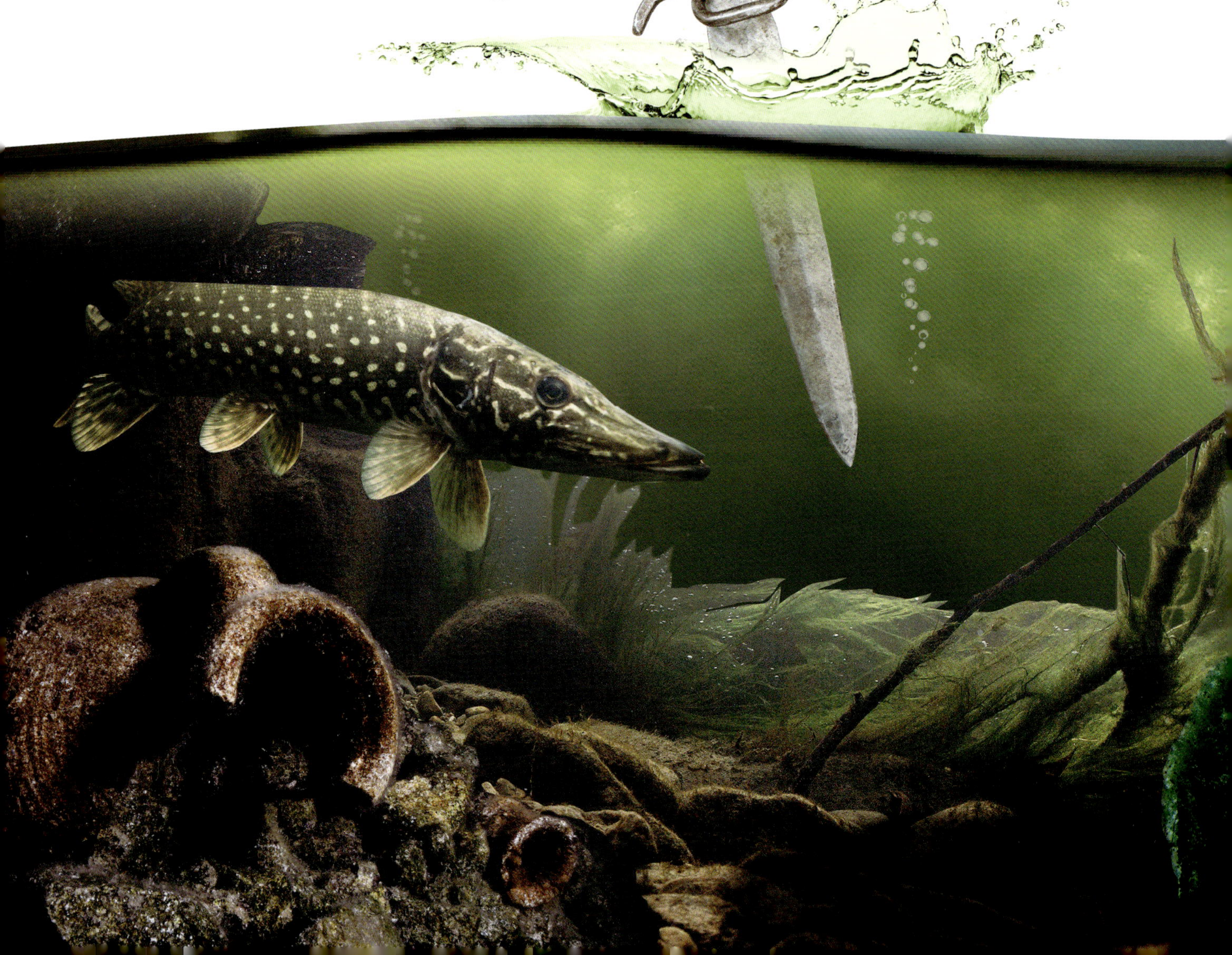

MAKING A CHOICE

39 FROM 127

Turning away from the open trapdoor, you trip over something in your hurry to leave the room. Holding up your lamp, you see two objects lying on the floor – a tinderbox and a length of chain. You decide to take one of these items with you.

STRIKING A LIGHT

A tinderbox containing a firesteel, flint and 'tinder' (dry straw or bark) is used to light a fire or candle from scratch. Fire is very important in the castle. It is needed to cook food, and to provide much-needed warmth and light.

Which do you choose?

▶ The tinderbox .... GO TO **77**

▶ The length of chain .... GO TO **51**

Chain *Tinderbox*

THE OTHER SIDE

40 FROM 14

You lower yourself into the water again, gagging at the horrible smell and trying not to think about what is under your feet. Swimming as fast as you can, you reach the other side of the moat and scramble out. Grabbing your shoes and the dagger, you sprint towards the woods near the drawbridge.

▶ .... GO TO **56**

TOP TABLE

41 FROM 58

As jesters juggle and musicians perform, you help to carry trays of pottage, a thick stew, to the guests. Your sister is seated at the top table and is obviously considered very important.

Do you dare speak to her?

➤ Yes, she surely has an important message for you .... **GO TO 17**

➤ No, you are dressed as a servant and not allowed to talk to guests ...... **GO TO 90**

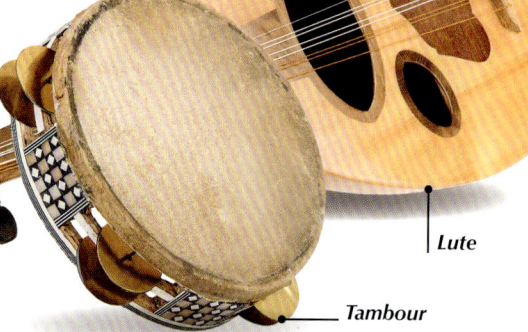

Lute

Tambour

A SHOVE

42 FROM 63, 97

The guard reaches the landing and pushes at the door. Rushing from your hiding place, you shove him hard into the room. His sword clatters to the ground and you seize it. As he whirls round, you hold its pointed tip to his chest and he steps back. You leave quickly and lock the door again.

➤ .... **GO TO 30**

ENTERTAINING THE GUESTS

Musicians called troubadours travel from town to town and castle to castle. They are paid to entertain people with their songs and tales. The instruments they play include the lute, tambour, bells, cymbals and recorder.

HELMET FIRST!

43 FROM 32, 83

A knight's armour is put on from bottom to top. Look at the suit of armour near Step 32 and try again!

Which order is it?

➤ Sabatons, greaves, breastplate, helmet .... **GO TO 119**

➤ Breastplate, helmet, sabatons, greaves .... **GO TO 83**

A DISGUISE

44 FROM 18, 30

At the bottom of the spiral staircase, you can hear faint shouts from the guards above. It will be a while before anyone notices something amiss. You spot a small room with a burning lamp on a table. Stepping inside, you find a large chest filled with clothing – a servant's tunic and cap, a jester's colourful garments and a noble's long velvet cloak. You guess the costumes belong to travelling entertainers. A disguise will help you to move around unnoticed.

How do you dress?

- As a servant in a tunic and cap .... **GO TO 8**
- In a jester's colourful garments .... **GO TO 102**
- As a noble in a long velvet cloak .... **GO TO 110**

CASTLE CHARACTERS

The castle is home to many people, from nobles and soldiers to entertainers and servants. The nobles wear fine clothes made of rich fabrics such as velvet. The servants wear simple peasant clothing made from coarse wool or hemp. The jester has a brightly coloured outfit and often wears a hat with bells on it.

DEEP WELL

45 FROM **25**

Peering down into the well, you can just make out some small steps cut into the thick wall of the well – might they lead all the way down and out? You're desperate to escape before you're caught and someone has just come out into the courtyard from the kitchen. Do you climb into the well?

CONSULT THE WHEEL
Turn to the knight symbol.

HELP

46 FROM **59**

As you hide, the archer stops to ask the alchemist if he's seen anyone. He replies that someone ran downstairs. When the archer has gone, the alchemist says, 'I helped you. Now, can you help me solve this puzzle?'

Alchemists use symbols to represent different elements. Can you work out which ones are missing in the puzzle below?

THE FOUR MAIN ALCHEMY SYMBOLS

EARTH AIR
FIRE   WATER

GO TO **52**

A LIE

47 FROM 108

You calmly place the dagger back on the table and tell the blacksmith you were just admiring his craft! To distract him, you ask him how long it took to make such a fine weapon. He stares hard at you for several seconds, then tells you to go away.

GO TO **6**

Practical weaponry
Daggers are useful weapons. They are also used for everyday reasons, for example, cutting food at the table.

A LOCKED TRAPDOOR

48 FROM 93

The child leaves and takes the lamp with her, so you are left in darkness. You need to hurry now because your sister will be leaving the castle. Taking out your candle and the tinderbox, you manage to strike a light. Looking around, you find a small trapdoor, but your heart sinks when you realise it's locked! Then you spot a key hanging on the back of the door you came through . . .

GO TO **84**

HOW TO LIGHT A CANDLE
1. Strike the flint against the firesteel to create sparks. Allow the sparks to fall on the tinder.
2. When a spark starts to smoulder, blow on it until you have a flame.
3. Transfer the flame to your candle.

Firesteel   *Flint*   *Tinder*

49 FROM 27, 130

SOLDIERS

As you enter the tower, you see several people filing down the stairs. You realise the tower must be used by the garrison, the soldiers that guard the castle, and turn to leave. Then you notice several more soldiers approaching from the courtyard behind you. You have no choice but to slip into the nearest room, a large armoury full of gleaming armour and weapons. To your horror, a knight follows you in.

➤ .... GO TO **32**

Halberd
Soldiers on foot use the halberd to bring down horsemen in battle.

DEFENDING THE CASTLE
The soldiers and knights who live in a castle and defend it are called the garrison. The number of men serving in the garrison depends on whether it is a time of peace or unrest.

Shield
These are often decorated, sometimes with the coat of arms of a noble family.

CHAIN

51 FROM 39

You pick up the heavy chain, but as you head for the door, it drags on the floor making a loud noise. You put the chain down and pick up the tinderbox. It will be more useful – being able to light a candle will help you see better. Where should you go now?

CONSULT THE WHEEL
Turn to the helmet symbol.

WHICH WAY?

52 FROM 46

Having solved the puzzle (the answers are Air, Fire, Water), you return to the battlements. Suddenly, you spot another archer to the right, who is moving in your direction. You walk the other way, but that is towards the guard whose mug of ale you took earlier.

What do you do?

▶ Walk past quickly and hope the guard doesn't ask any questions .... GO TO **111**

▶ Hide by pressing yourself into the gap by an arrowslit .... GO TO **75**

HIT FROM BEHIND

50 FROM 34

You start walking downstairs, but the sound of voices below makes you turn back. Peering along the wall walk, you decide to turn right. All seems quiet. But you've only taken a few steps when you feel a sharp pain in your back – you've been hit by an arrow! Injured, you crumple to the ground.

That's the end of your escape quest. But you did well to make it this far. Perhaps you'll make it out next time if you dare to start the adventure again.

▶ If you do .... GO TO **1**

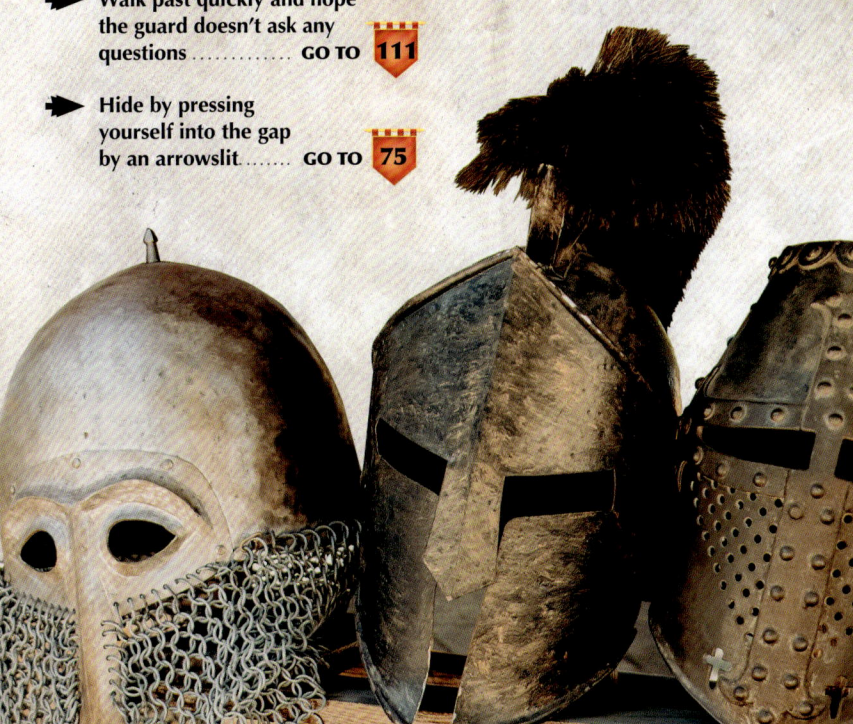

TREASURE CHEST

53 FROM **2, 10**

Are you sure? Look closely at the words in Step 10 and think again.

What is the answer?

➤ An egg .... GO TO **61**

➤ A maze .... GO TO **2**

NO WAY OUT

55 FROM **127**

You climb down the rope. Then disaster! The rotten rope suddenly breaks, and you tumble into the black pit. You're not too badly hurt, but your light has gone out. You can't climb back out and if you call for help, you'll only be recaptured.

That's the end of your escape quest. You only got a little way through the medieval castle!

➤ If you dare to start the adventure again .... GO TO **1**

POTIONS

54 FROM **29**

You flee down the steps. As you reach the first floor, you glimpse a small room. Inside, an alchemist is standing over a table covered in plants and potion bottles. If you go inside, the pursuing archer might run straight past and down the stairs. Do you go in?

CONSULT THE WHEEL
Turn to the stars symbol.

Tools of the trade
The alchemist's workshop is full of flasks and crucibles containing the materials he needs.

SECRET SIGNAL

56 FROM 40

You're not safe yet! But then you hear the familiar snort of a horse and realise Alianor is in the woods. Crawling into the trees, you give a low owl's hoot – the signal you have both used since you were small children. Your sister appears from the shadows and helps you up onto her horse. You have escaped the castle!

Mixing elements
Alchemists mix and heat salts, acids and other chemicals in their experiments.

FINDING INFORMATION

57 FROM 23, 106, 129

As the guard seizes his prize, you wonder if you can trick the pair into giving away information. First you praise the castle's design, and the guards proudly agree, boasting of the deep moat that defends its entrance. Then you say that the problem with such a well-built castle is that it would be impossible for anyone to escape during a siege! 'Not true,' one of them replies. 'The Lord's Tower has a way out.' It may be dangerous to ask more questions.

What do you do?

➤ Tell the guards you must return to your duties .... **GO TO 130**

➤ Find out more about the Lord's Tower .... **GO TO 72**

THE MAGIC OF ALCHEMY
Alchemists mix mysterious potions in the hope of finding the 'philosopher's stone', a substance they believe can change ordinary metals into precious gold or silver. They believe that when they find it, they will be able to cure any illness and help people to live forever.

58 FROM 20, 81, 118

A WELCOME SIGHT

You remember the order correctly. A richly dressed lady holds out her hands to be washed. As you pour water over them, she leans close and urgently whispers, 'Don't you know me?' Looking up, you're amazed to see that it is your older sister Alianor! But there's no time to speak now – a bugle sounds and the lord and lady of the castle enter the hall.

▶ .... **GO TO 41**

59 FROM 54

A RISK

As you burst into the room, the startled alchemist looks up. You hide behind the door and beg his silence by placing your finger to your lips. But are you able to trust him?

CONSULT THE WHEEL
Turn to the unicorn symbol.

Homegrown drinks
Pitchers of wine or cider are served wherever grapes or apples and pears are grown.

Pastry dishes
Meat and fish pies, as well as sweet pies and pastries, are very popular.

A truckle of cheese

Eggy treat
Boiled eggs are served whole, or are sometimes stuffed with food, such as fish roe.

STRICT SEATING ORDER
The lord, the lady and their most important guests sit on chairs at the top table, which is often on a dais, or raised platform. Other guests are seated on benches according to their rank, with those of higher birth closer to the top table.

60 FROM 75

NOWHERE TO HIDE?

You nervously crouch down. You'll surely be seen by whoever is coming round the corner and your mind buzzes as you try to think of a solution. Could you quickly lower yourself into the deep, smelly shaft beneath the garderobe to hide? You know it leads all the way down to the moat – and it's a long way to fall if you lose your grip!

Do you?

➤ Stay crouching down................ **GO TO 92**

➤ Lower yourself down the shaft....... **GO TO 115**

Golden goblet
In the richest castles, goblets made of gold are used at the high table.

Mead
This honey wine may be either still or sparkling.

A FEAST AT THE FEAST

Castle feasts often start with a pottage, a type of stew or soup, followed by a variety of meat and fish dishes, and savoury and sweet pies. People use knives and spoons (no forks), and eat with their hands. Slabs of stale bread called trenchers are used as plates.

Roast meats
There is always a vast range of meats including chicken, pheasant, goose and duck.

GLEAMING WEAPON

61 FROM 2, 10, 53

You got it right and the jingling jester bows to let you continue on your way. Across the courtyard you pass a workshop. Glancing inside, you see a blacksmith hard at work. His back is turned as he hammers hot metal, while a freshly forged dagger lies on a table behind him. A weapon would be useful, but if you take it, the blacksmith might see you.

Do you pick up the dagger?

▶ No, who knows what the blacksmith will do if he catches you stealing ..... **GO TO 6**

▶ Yes, you may need to defend yourself later .... **GO TO 108**

IN THE FORGE

The blacksmith plays a vital role in castle life, making important tools, armour and weapons. His skill is highly valued though sometimes seen as a form of magic or witchcraft. For this reason, although he is well respected, he is also feared.

CLINGING ON

62 FROM 112

Climbing over the wall, you lower yourself down and hang onto the battlements for dear life. You try not to look but it's a long way down to the moat below! It's getting harder to hold on – and slowly your fingers lose their grip . . .

This is the end of your escape quest. You did well!

▶ If you dare to start the adventure again .... **GO TO** 1

CHANGE OF HEART

63 FROM 97

Your mind races as you rush downstairs. You'll surely be caught when the watchman raises the alarm – of course, you must try and lock him up! You go back and hide around the corner just in time!

▶ .... **GO TO** 42

CREEPY CRYPT

64 FROM 65

You run down the steps into the small crypt where you see two stone coffins. You instantly realise your mistake – there's nowhere else to go! The priest locks the door, and you find yourself in total blackness.

That's the end of your escape quest. You didn't get very far through the medieval castle!

➤ If you dare to start the adventure again .... **GO TO 1**

UNDER THE CHAPEL
A crypt is a dark stone chamber beneath the floor of a chapel or church that contains the tombs of important people. Their stone coffins are often surrounded by relics, which are the personal items of saints or religious people that are believed to have special powers.

BAD DECISION

The priest smiles unpleasantly and you realise you've made a terrible mistake! 'Do you really think I would betray my lord?' he asks as he calls for a guard.

Do you?

- Try to persuade him to help .... GO TO **94**
- Run back to the great hall .... GO TO **107**
- Run down to the crypt below .... GO TO **64**

LOCKED IN!

Pushing the girl away, you step into the little room and close the door. The woman comes into the lord's chamber and asks the child if she's been playing in the secret room again. Then she says she's going to lock it! A few seconds later, you hear a turning key. You're trapped and are bound to be found by the lord himself!

That's the end of your escape quest. But you did very well to make it this far through the medieval castle. Perhaps you'll make it out next time if you dare to start again.

- If you do ...... GO TO **1**

SHADOW

The footsteps behind you are now just around the corner, so you open the door and slip in, then quietly shut it. You are immediately struck by how cold it is in the small room. You warily move your light around and start with fright – there's a shadow in the corner! You've heard the castle is haunted. Is this the ghost? Then you realise that the shadow is being made by an open trapdoor.

Are you brave enough to take a look?

CONSULT THE WHEEL
Turn to the lion symbol.

BACK TO THE DUNGEON

The priest chases you all the way to the dungeon. As he lunges to grab you, you push him into the pit and shut the trapdoor. It will be a while before anyone hears his muffled cries! You decide to head to the courtyard – perhaps there's a way out there?

GO TO 25

BEWARE – GUARD!

You turn right. You're now incredibly hungry and take a pie from your pocket. Eating as you walk, you hurry along the battlements. Rounding a corner, you find a guard with his back turned. There's a mug of ale nearby. The pie has made you thirsty – should you risk taking a drink as you pass?

Keeping watch
Guards patrol the battlements, on the alert for enemy attack.

 **CONSULT THE WHEEL**
Turn to the crossed axes symbol.

SAFE TO DRINK
Ale is a type of beer. It is drunk by almost everyone, including children. It is safer to drink than water, which often contains deadly germs!

TRAPPED

70 FROM 5

As you round the final step, you see moonlight falling through the bars of an iron grille. Beyond, you see thick undergrowth leading out to a small bank and the castle moat. You press at the bars but the grille doesn't budge! Then you hear the sound of the trapdoor above opening – someone's coming!

What should you do?

➤ Keep trying to open the grille .... **GO TO** 120

➤ Rush up the steps and try to push past whoever is coming down .... **GO TO** 76

RETREAT

71 FROM 14

You run back through the open grille, just as the fallen guard rises shakily to his feet. You've been caught!

That's the end of your escape quest. You almost did it!

➤ Perhaps you'll make it out next time if you dare to start the adventure again .... **GO TO** 1

MORE QUESTIONS

72 FROM 57

You start by asking the guard if he has ever been inside the Lord's Tower. 'Of course!' he replies. 'But why do you ask?' You realise he's getting suspicious, so you stop your questions and tell him you must return to your duties.

➤ .... **GO TO** 130

INTO THE DARKNESS

73 FROM 8

You quickly and quietly run away from the footsteps down the dark passage. It's just as well you have a light! But what if someone has followed you? You come to a wall and turn sharp left. A short passage leads to a door. Dare you go through? There may be guards inside. But it may also lead to a way out of the castle. Then you hear the footsteps getting closer.

GO TO **67**

SPIDERWEBS

74 FROM **121**

You continue clambering down the well, spiderwebs brushing against your face. Suddenly you lose your footing and tumble down, bouncing off the slippery walls.

That's the end of your escape quest.

▶ If you dare to start the adventure again .... GO TO **1**

A CLOSE SHAVE

75 FROM **52, 113**

Your heart beats wildly as you press yourself into the space by the arrowslit, but the archer walks past. After a few minutes, you peek out. There is no one in view and you run to the next tower. But as you pass through its door, you hear footsteps from below. You daren't turn back, so you slip into the tiny garderobe containing a toilet which is built into the wall.

▶ .... GO TO **60**

A TUMBLE

76 FROM **70**

You rush up the steps and the person coming down tries to grab you. You give them a hard shove and they tumble down the steps. Should you carry on going up the steps? Or might it be better to go back down to the grille?

Which way should you go?

▶ Back down to the grille .... GO TO **131**

▶ Up to the lord's chamber .... GO TO **82**

BUSY SERVANT

77 FROM **39, 51**

Putting the tinderbox in your pocket, you leave the room and move quietly back down the now-empty passage. You reach the great hall where tables are being prepared for a feast. But your candle has now burnt out and you will need a new one to light the castle's dark passages. You spot an unlit one on a table, but there is a servant there. You passed a chapel on the way. Should you look there instead?

LIGHTING THE WAY

Tallow candles are cheap but produce a smoky flame and a horrible smell. Beeswax candles do not produce smoke and last much longer. But they are expensive and are usually kept for church ceremonies.

Do you?

➤ Take the servant's candle .... **GO TO 98**

➤ Look for the chapel .... **GO TO 35**

PRIEST

78 FROM **109**

Emerging from your hiding place, you explain to the shocked priest that you're an innocent prisoner who needs help. Will he help you or will he betray you to the guards?

➤ .... **GO TO 65**

RISK

79 FROM **21**

You turn back and start feeling your way up the broken steps. But you quickly realise there's little chance of escape if you return to the lord's chamber. You decide you must take a risk and find out what lies at the bottom of the dark stairs.

➤ .... **GO TO 5**

THE GREAT HALL

This is the heart of the castle and its main gathering place. It is used for everyday activities, such as eating and sleeping, and for grand feasts. Other important places, such as the kitchen and the chapel, are nearby.

SPARKLING GIFT

80 FROM 28, 88, 104

You slip the ring on your thumb – it will make a wonderful gift for your mother! When you lift the dagger out, you find another key. Putting the dagger in your pocket, you return to the hidden room and try the key – it works! Prising open the trapdoor, you find a narrow staircase spiralling down into deep blackness. You hear voices and realise there's no time to lose! Should you climb down?

 **CONSULT THE WHEEL**
Turn to the crossed swords symbol.

BASIN, KNIFE, NAPKIN

81 FROM 20, 118

Are you sure? Think carefully and make your choice again.

Which are the three things?

➤ Ewer, basin, napkin .... **GO TO 58**

➤ Basin, spoon, knife .... **GO TO 20**

BREASTPLATE FIRST

83 FROM 32, 43

A knight's armour is put on from bottom to top. Look at the suit of armour near Step 32 and try again.

What is the order?

➤ Sabatons, greaves, breastplate, helmet .... **GO TO 119**

➤ Helmet, greaves sabatons, breastplate .... **GO TO 43**

DILEMMA

82 FROM 76

You return to the lord's chamber and look for a candle. Then you hear footsteps and urgent voices nearby. It's clear more people are looking for you!

What do you do?

➤ Return to the grille .... **GO TO 131**

➤ Hide in the treasure chest .... **GO TO 89**

MYSTERY KEY

84 FROM 48

It's soon obvious that the key is too big for the trapdoor, but it might open the chest in the lord's bedchamber. You try it in the lock. Does it fit?

 **CONSULT THE WHEEL**
Turn to the three keys symbol.

85 FROM 29 — PET DOG

Thinking quickly, you tell the archer that one of the guests at the feast has lost a pet dog and you've been asked to look for it. The archer laughs mockingly. 'There's no pet dog up on the battlements! Go back the way you came!'

➡ .... GO TO 111

87 FROM 91, 101 — BREATH

Other people don't use breath any more than you do! Look at the riddle in Step 101 and try again.

What is the answer?

➡ Money .... GO TO 91

➡ Your name .... GO TO 7

86 FROM 37, 105 — A MIGHTY THROW

You hurl the dagger with all your strength. It lands blade-side down in the mud on the other side of the moat.

➡ .... GO TO 14

88 FROM 84

GLINTING GEMS

The chest opens and you are overjoyed to see the glint of your mother's dagger! You also find a heavy gold crown, a magnificent sword and a ruby-set ring. You decide you can carry the dagger and one more item, as long as it is not too heavy.

Which do you choose?

➤ The sword .... GO TO **28**
➤ The ring .... GO TO **80**
➤ The crown .... GO TO **104**

The lord's sword

Gold crown

Ruby-set ring

A SAFE PLACE

The locked chest is where the lord and lady keep their most treasured possessions. One of the most important is the lord's sword, which has been specially made for him or perhaps handed down through the generations. A symbol of bravery and honour, the weapon is up to 80 cm in length – as long as a knight's leg!

89 DUST
FROM 82

You just manage to fit into the treasure chest and lower the lid. Someone comes into the room and starts moving about. Then some dust catches in your throat and you can't help but splutter. The lid is yanked open, and the lord's son looks down on you in triumph.

That's the end of your escape quest. But you did very well to make it this far through the medieval castle. Perhaps you'll make it out next time.

▶ If you dare to start again .... GO TO 1

90 KING ARTHUR
FROM 17, 41

As you retreat, a troubadour starts to tell an exciting tale about King Arthur and the Knights of the Round Table. As the guests listen, you make eye contact with Alianor. She nods in the direction of the doorway, as if telling you to leave the hall. You're not sure if you've understood – you tell yourself that if you can remember the name of King Arthur's magical sword (before the troubadour mentions it), you will leave. If you can't, you will stay.

What is the name?

▶ Lancelot .... GO TO 11
▶ Excalibur .... GO TO 36
▶ Guinevere .... GO TO 15

TELLING TALES
As well as singing and playing instruments, troubadours entertain the castle guests with stories about heroic battles and great knights. Some of the most popular stories told are those about King Arthur, his queen Guinevere, his magical sword Excalibur and the Knights of the Round Table.

An Irish bouzouki, a type of lute

MONEY

91 FROM 87, 101

Money has weight! Look at the riddle in Step 101 and try again.

What is the answer?
➤ Breath .... GO TO **87**
➤ Your name .... GO TO **7**

VOICES

92 FROM 60

You stay crouching down, but you freeze when you hear voices. Someone says your name – are they discussing your escape? It would be foolish to stay where you are, so you quickly return to the toilet in the garderobe and climb into the shaft.

➤ .... GO TO **115**

HIDE-AND-SEEK

93 FROM 126

In the little room, you tell the girl it's a game. The woman enters the bedchamber and calls out again. When she's gone, you tell the girl to leave, but to say nothing about you. Does she do as you ask?

CONSULT THE WHEEL

Turn to the rose symbol.

PILLORIED!

94 FROM 65

You are caught and dragged to the yard. As a punishment for stealing the candles, you are put in the pillory to be pelted with rotten food and mud.

That's the end of your escape quest. You can't escape the pillory.

▶ If you dare to start the adventure again .... **GO TO 1**

AT THE PILLORY
A pillory is used to punish crimes such as dishonesty and stealing. The culprit's neck and wrists are held fast between wooden boards, while a crowd mocks them and pelts them with rotten food or mud.

Missiles
Rotten fruit and vegetables are thrown to punish a thief.

LUCKY ESCAPE

95 FROM 3

As the dog leaps and snarls at you, several flapping ravens appear to ward it off. The dog seems afraid of them, and you decide to offer it the second meat pie.

▶ .... **GO TO 125**

TINKLING BELLS

96 FROM 102

As you move down the corridor, the bells on the jester's hat start to tinkle. They will draw attention, so you need to return and choose a different outfit.

Which one is best?

▶ The servant's tunic and cap .... **GO TO 8**

▶ The noble's long velvet cloak .... **GO TO 110**

WHAT NOW?

97 FROM 1

You find yourself on a small landing. A narrow staircase spirals away, up and down. You know there are one or two watchmen in the turret above, and now you can hear someone coming down the stairs. He will surely raise the alarm. Should you just run for it? Or could you possibly lock him in with the other guard to gain precious time? You would need to silently unlock the door, hide just around the corner and wait for him to walk into the room.

Do you?

▶ Unlock the door, then hide and wait .... **GO TO 42**

▶ Run quickly away down the steps .... **GO TO 63**

NICE TRY

98 FROM 77

You creep up behind the servant, who is arranging one of the tables. You hope he won't notice as you reach for the candle, but he whips around and snaps, 'Don't take that – I need it!' He looks at you suspiciously. You apologise and turn around – can you escape to the chapel before he raises the alarm?

CONSULT THE WHEEL

Turn to the dragon symbol.

A SLIPPERY SLIDE

99 FROM 115

You slowly push yourself down the stinky shaft. Will you get stuck? Then suddenly the shaft widens, and you start to slide very fast, hitting the moat with an enormous splash. As you bob up to the surface, you see the lord staring in amazement from the drawbridge.

That's the end of your escape quest. But you did well to make it this far through the medieval castle. Perhaps you'll make it out next time.

▶ If you dare to start the adventure again .... **GO TO 1**

100 FRIGHT!
FROM 9

You hear something moving in the corner. Is this the ghost you've heard about? No, it's a raven and it is swooping towards you! You're desperate to get away from its flapping wings and find a way out of the castle, but a dog is now barking at the foot of the stairs. A loud voice tells it to climb up. The dog growls savagely as it bounds up the steps to the top.

What do you do?

- Hide in the shadows, unsure of what may be lurking there ...... **GO TO 3**
- Take out the second meat pie and hope you can calm the dog .... **GO TO 125**

101 A RIDDLE
FROM 24, 122

You discover the girl has been made to stay away from the feast as a punishment for climbing a tree and tearing her clothes. Offering her the sweet pie from your bag, you ask what her favourite things are. 'Riddles!' she replies. Then she asks, 'Can you answer this one?'

*'There is something precious that you own,
Though other people use it more than you do.
You carry it everywhere you go,
But it doesn't weigh a thing!'*

What is it?

- Money .... **GO TO 91**
- Breath .... **GO TO 87**
- Your name .... **GO TO 7**

102 THE JESTER'S COSTUME
FROM 44

You pull on the jester's bright clothes and step out of the room.

- .... **GO TO 96**

A FALL

103 FROM 110

As you walk along the corridor, your feet get tangled in the long cloak and you fall over. You crash to the ground and guards come running – you are caught!

That's the end of your escape quest. You didn't get far through the medieval castle.

▶ If you dare to start the adventure again .... GO TO **1**

GOLD CROWN

104 FROM 28, 88

You place the crown on your head but it's very heavy. It will be tricky to carry it out of the castle and across the moat! You put it back and select another object instead.

What do you choose?

▶ Ring .... GO TO **80**

▶ Sword .... GO TO **28**

SHOES OFF

105 FROM 120

You know there's no time to lose. But before you can swim, you'll have to lose certain items. You quickly remove your shoes and hurl them across to the other side. They only just reach dry land! You are wearing the ring, but the precious dagger is much heavier.

What do you do?

▶ Risk throwing the dagger across the moat .... GO TO **86**

▶ Carry the dagger and hope it does not weigh you down ...... GO TO **37**

YOU

106 FROM 23, 129

Wrong! Take a look at the Raffle rules near Step 23 and think again.

Who is the winner?

➡ Guard one .... GO TO **129**

➡ Guard two .... GO TO **57**

RUN FOR IT!

107 FROM 65

You sprint towards the hall, the priest right behind you. There's no one there. Perhaps you could lead the priest all the way down to the room with the open trapdoor and push him into the dungeon. Or you could just try to trip him up.

Do you?

➡ Run to the dungeon .... GO TO **68**

➡ Try to trip up the priest .... GO TO **116**

THIEF!

108 FROM 61

You creep up behind the blacksmith and quietly reach for the dagger. Just as you pick it up, the blacksmith whips round and glares at you. 'Stop, thief!' he yells.

What is your next move?

➡ Put the dagger back and tell him you're just looking .... GO TO **47**

➡ Make for the nearby stables and hide .... GO TO **16**

MORNING PRAYERS

109 FROM 35

You dive into the small space beneath the stone altar and nervously wait. Someone comes in and you see the long robes of a priest as he stands before the altar. He is clearly preparing for morning prayers. Should you ask for his help? Or maybe he's so busy that he won't notice if you creep out of the chapel into the courtyard.

What do you do?

- Crawl round the altar and out of the chapel .... GO TO **25**
- Ask the priest to help you .... GO TO **78**

TRUSTED PRIEST

The priest leads all the religious services in the castle chapel. He writes all the lord's letters, and often teaches the castle children how to read and write. He is much trusted by the lord and lady and is very loyal to them.

THE VELVET CLOAK

110 FROM 44, 96

You wrap the noble's velvet cloak around yourself and step out of the room.

 .... GO TO **103**

SPOTTED!

111 FROM 52, 85

With your heart beating hard, you retrace your steps past the guard. But only a few steps along, he commands you to stop, and then to empty your pockets. You bring out the stolen ale mug and you are grabbed by the scruff of your neck and marched away.

This is the end of your escape quest. You did very well!

- If you dare to start the adventure again .... GO TO **1**

A CAGE

112 FROM 124

You turn left and move along the wall walk. But the barking is now much closer! Peering over the battlements, you see a cage hanging from the wall with a prisoner inside. You know that only the worst criminals are punished like this. You need to hide, so you climb over. But is it safer to cling to the cage or to the crumbling castle wall?

Do you?

➤ Cling onto the cage .... **GO TO 19**

➤ Cling to the battlements .... **GO TO 62**

A QUICK DRINK

113 FROM 69

Tiptoeing past the distracted guard, you grab the mug of ale and continue along the wall walk. At a safe distance, you thirstily gulp down the liquid and put the mug in your pocket. Suddenly, you spot two archers ahead. They haven't seen you yet, but they probably know there's a prisoner on the run. Maybe they won't notice you. Or perhaps you can find a place to hide?

What should you do?

➤ Keep going and hope they don't see you .... **GO TO 29**

➤ Hide by pressing into the hollow of the arrowslit .... **GO TO 75**

ARROWSLITS

There are narrow gaps called arrowslits in the hollowed-out spaces of the battlements that run round the top of the castle wall. They give cover to the archers, allowing them to fire through the slim gaps. The archers can take aim without being seen by an enemy.

A LOUD NOISE

114 FROM **125**

You decide to go down to the wall walk and move along the battlements in the dwindling light. As you near the Lord's Tower, you see a watchman guarding the door. Luckily, there's a cannon close by and you dart behind it. Then, taking the ale mug from your bag, you hurl it as far as you can along the way you've just come. As you hoped, the loud clatter brings the guard running. Once he's passed, you run as fast as you can into the tower.

▶ .... GO TO **122**

Cannons
These fired iron cannonballs at enemy soldiers.

A HORRIBLE STENCH

115 FROM **60, 92**

You cling to the edge of the slimy shaft and try not to be sick at the smell. The footsteps pause outside the garderobe – the chamber that houses the toilet – and you hardly dare to breathe. After several long seconds, they walk on. As you prepare to scramble out, you have a thought. Would it be possible to clamber down the shaft and escape the castle that way or might you fall or get stuck?

What do you do?

▶ Start climbing down the smelly shaft .... GO TO **99**

▶ Get out – what if you get stuck or fall? .... GO TO **34**

CAPTURED!

116 FROM **107**

As the priest pursues you through the hall, you turn round and trip him up with your foot. His roars of pain bring several servants running. Joining the chase, they soon drag you to the ground.

That's the end of your escape quest. You didn't get very far through the medieval castle!

▶ If you dare to start the adventure again .... GO TO **1**

RUMBLING STOMACH

117 FROM 128

You look around as you push yourself out of the well. Everyone is too busy to notice you. Your stomach is growling. Should you head for the busy kitchen? Some food might help you think clearly.

 **CONSULT THE WHEEL**
Turn to the crown symbol.

Ewer

Basin
The water may be perfumed.

FEAST ETIQUETTE

118 FROM 13

Two hours later, you are hot and dirty but the meat is cooked. You wash and help to carry pitchers of wine and ale into the great hall. Then one of the stewards instructs you to help wash the hands of the guests before the midday meal. You think you can remember what to do – after all, you've seen this ritual performed many times – but what three things will you need to carry out the task?

What do you need?

➤ Ewer, basin, napkin............ **GO TO 58**

➤ Basin, spoon, knife............ **GO TO 20**

➤ Basin, knife, napkin............ **GO TO 81**

RITUAL FOR THE GUESTS

Before and after a meal, servants wash the hands of the most important guests. Holding ewers, or jugs, they pour warm water over their hands into a basin, then pass them a napkin. Less important guests wash their own hands at basins on a table near the doors.

Napkin *Knife* *Spoon*

WORRYING NEWS

119 FROM 32, 43, 83

Luckily, you remember the correct order and help the knight put on his heavy armour. You're shocked to hear from him that the guards are hunting for an escaped prisoner, with a dog! You decide that as soon as he leaves, you'll head up the tower to the battlements.

▶ .... GO TO **124**

OUT!

120 FROM 70, 131

You push the grille with all your strength, and it shifts and gives way. You clamber into thick undergrowth and desperately push your way through. You are standing on a tiny bank. Beyond, there are woods and to your right the drawbridge – but first you need to get across the icy moat.

▶ .... GO TO **105**

A SLIPPERY DESCENT

121 FROM 45

You lower your legs to the first foothold. As you descend, it gets darker and darker. You're afraid of heights and the walls are slippery with moss. It's becoming difficult to cling on.

Do you?

▶ Climb back up – better safe than sorry .... GO TO **128**

▶ Keep going, despite the slippery walls .... GO TO **74**

A YOUNG CHILD

122 FROM 114

Finally, you are in the Lord's Tower where you will hopefully find the way out the guards spoke about. You head down to the next level and along a corridor. Looking in one of the doors, you see a large room dimly lit by firelight. There's a girl of around six who seems to be alone. Next to her is a board game, and she's crying loudly. You worry her sobs may attract attention.

What do you do?

➤ Befriend the girl and get her help .... **GO TO 101**

➤ Carry on looking for the way out on your own .... **GO TO 24**

DOG CHASE

123 FROM 3

Leaping up from the shadows, you just manage to pass the snapping dog. But you're only halfway down the staircase when you feel its teeth pulling at your tunic. As you fall, the dog's master comes bounding up the steps. You're a prisoner again!

That's the end of your escape quest. But you did well to make it this far through the medieval castle. Perhaps you'll make it out next time.

➤ If you dare to start your adventure again .... **GO TO 1**

FAMILY ROOM
The solar is a room above ground level that is used as a private living area by the lord and lady and their children. In the summer months, it is lit and warmed by sunlight, but in winter candles and a wood fire are needed.

Board games
Chess and draughts are popular games for all the family.

Draughts checkerboard

BARKING DOG

124 FROM 119

The knight heads out to joust, so you quickly climb the tower and come out into the open air. You're now on the wall walk leading right around the castle on top of the battlements. On the far side, there's a raised flag on one of the towers. Surely that must be the Lord's Tower and the way out of the castle? It would be quicker to go left, but you think you can hear a dog's distant barks coming from that direction . . .

Do you?

➤ Go right, away from the barking dog .... **GO TO 69**

➤ Go left, towards the barking dog .... **GO TO 112**

WORKING DOGS

A dog keeper trains and looks after the castle dogs. Greyhounds, mastiffs and Irish wolfhounds are kept for hunting and as guard dogs. Nobles can afford to keep dogs as pets, and lords and ladies often have small, faithful dogs at their side.

GROWLS AND SNARLS

125 FROM 95, 100

'Here,' you whisper soothingly and hold out the remaining meat pie. The snarling dog moves suspiciously towards your hand and snatches the treat. As it gulps it down, its master calls and the dog obediently trots away. Soon the voices fade into the distance. But is it safe to leave the tower yet?

CONSULT THE WHEEL
Turn to the dog symbol.

IN THE CHAMBER
The lord and lady of the castle have the rare luxury of privacy. The lord's chamber has a four-poster bed with curtains to keep out cold draughts. A rich tapestry hangs on the wall, and valuable possessions are kept in a locked chest.

THE LORD'S CHAMBER

126 FROM 7

Inside the bedchamber, you see a big chest. You ask what it contains and the girl tells you it's always locked! Then, laughing, she slips behind a large wall tapestry and shows you a tiny door leading into a small room. Maybe this is the way out! Just then, a woman's voice calls the child's name.

Do you?

➤ Whisper that you should both hide in the secret room .... **GO TO 93**

➤ Hide in the secret room on your own .... **GO TO 66**

Tapestry
Tapestries hang on the stone walls both for decoration and to keep the room warm.

Chest

BRAVE MOVE

127 FROM 22

Taking your courage in both hands, you peer into the gloom again. As your eyes become accustomed to the dark, you see a rat moving away from the skeleton. Not the ghost after all! Then you hear a noise outside in the passageway. Should you climb down the rope hanging from the trapdoor? The rope looks a little rotten but this may be a good hiding place.

Do you?

➤ Wait to see if the noise fades .... **GO TO 39**

➤ Climb down the rope .... **GO TO 55**

FOOD FOR THOUGHT

128 FROM 121

Reluctantly, you climb back up the well. Nearing the top, you hear voices and realise there are now people milling about the courtyard getting ready for the midday feast. Will they spot you?

➤ .... **GO TO 117**

GUARD ONE

129 FROM 23, 106

Wrong! Take a look at the Raffle rules near Step 23 and think again.

➤ You .... **GO TO 106**

➤ Guard two .... **GO TO 57**

NO TIME TO LOSE

130 FROM 57, 72

Walking away across the courtyard, you realise the guards may still raise the alarm, so you need to keep out of sight! To your right is one of the castle towers but you don't know what lies inside. To the left is a gate that leads to the heart of the castle, but there's a guard there.

What should you do next?

➡ Enter the castle tower.................... **GO TO 49**

➡ Go through the guarded gate into the inner castle............. **GO TO 27**

SAFE WALL WALK

The castle towers lead up to the battlements, a protective barrier around the top of the castle's outer walls. Inside the battlements is the wall walk that leads from tower to tower. Anyone walking along it cannot be seen from the courtyard below.

GRILLE

131 FROM 76, 82

You return to the grille and see a guard lying at the foot of the steps. He's been knocked out, but is still breathing. You need to hurry – the guard could wake up at any moment! Can you open the grille before he wakes up?

CONSULT THE WHEEL

Turn to the eagle symbol.

THE TRUE PATH THROUGH THE CASTLE

To get out of the medieval castle safely and in the shortest number of steps, you need to take the true path. To do that, judge each option carefully and use the clues in the pictures and captions to help you. If you get stuck, see the answers below.

1. **An Unexpected Turn!** Go to 97

2. **What Now?** Unlock the door, hide and wait for the guard. You must try and lock him up. If you run away, he'll raise the alarm and you'll be caught! Go to 42

3. **A Shove** Go to 30

4. **Which Way?** Go down the stairs to the courtyard. There's unlikely to be a way out from the high watchtower, and if you meet an armed person coming down, they will have space to swing their sword. Go to 44

5. **A Disguise** Choose the servant's tunic and cap. The simple clothing will mean you can move around without drawing attention to yourself. Go to 8

6. **Footsteps** Go to 73

7. **Into the Darkness** Go to 67

8. **Shadow** Go to 22

9. **Trapdoor** Go to 127

10. **Brave Move** Don't climb down the rope. If it breaks, you'll be stuck in the pit forever! Go to 39

11. **Making a Choice** Take the tinderbox. The castle has many dark passageways, and you won't be able to light a candle without it. Go to 77

12. **Busy Servant** Look for the chapel. The candles in there are made from beeswax, and do not produce as much smoke as tallow candles. You will be less likely to be noticed. Go to 35

13. **Looking for Light** Go to 109

14. **Morning Prayers** Crawl round the altar and out of the chapel. The priest is loyal to his lord and will turn you in if you ask him for help. Go to 25

15. **Into the Courtyard** Go to 45

16. **Deep Well** Go to 121

17. **A Slippery Descent** Climb back up the well. It's unlikely to lead to a way out of the castle and the walls are too slippery to hold on to. Go to 128

(18) **Food for Thought** Go to 117

(19) **Rumbling Stomach** Go to 4

(20) **Pies!** Apologise and put the pie back. If you run away, you're bound to be chased and may well be caught. Go to 13

(21) **A Lucky Escape** Go to 118

(22) **Feast Etiquette** You'll need the ewer, basin and napkin. Go to 58

(23) **A Welcome Sight** Go to 41

(24) **Top Table** No – if you speak to a guest at the top table while dressed as a servant, you'll draw attention to yourself and get into trouble! Go to 90

(25) **King Arthur** King Arthur's magical sword is called Excalibur. Go to 36

(26) **Secret Message** Go to 10

Reach the other side of the moat by the drawbridge. Hoot once.

(27) **Riddle-di-di** It's an egg. The white of the egg represents the castle, its shell is the castle wall, and the egg yolk is the golden treasure at the heart of the castle. Go to 61

(28) **Gleaming Weapon** No, don't pick up the dagger. Some say the blacksmith has magical powers and it would be foolish to risk his anger! Go to 6

(29) **The Gatehouse** Go to 12

(30) **A Bet** Use the last silver penny in your pocket. The guards are unlikely to be satisfied with a pie and they may think you've stolen it. Go to 23

(31) **A Game of Dice** The second guard is the winner. In the game of Raffle, the first person to throw three dice with the same number wins the bet. Go to 57

(32) **Finding Information** Tell the guards you must return to your duties. If you ask them more questions, they'll probably think you're up to no good. Go to 130

(33) **No Time to Lose** Enter the castle tower. It will take you up to the wall walk, which leads from tower to tower. You'll be able to look for the Lord's Tower and you won't be seen from the courtyard below. Go to 49

(34) **Soldiers** Go to 32

(35) **In the Armoury** Sabatons, greaves, breastplate, helmet. Armour is strapped on from bottom to top. Go to 119

(36) **Worrying News** Go to 124

(37) **Barking Dog** Go right, away from the barking. It won't be quicker to go left if you run into a savage dog! Go to 69

(38) **Beware – Guard** Go to 113

(39) **A Quick Drink** Hide by pressing into the hollow of the arrowslit. It's too risky to walk towards the archers ahead. Go to 75

(40) **A Close Shave** Go to 60

(41) **Nowhere to Hide?** Lower yourself down the shaft. You need to hide from the person coming and this is the only option. Go to 115

(42) **A Horrible Stench!** Get out of the narrow, slippery shaft. If you get stuck or injured in a fall, you'll never escape the castle! Go to 34

(43) **Arrow Attack** Go up the spiral staircase. The broken steps leading down look too risky, and you need to find cover quickly. Go to 9

(44) **Abandoned Tower** Go to 100

(45) **Fright!** Take out the meat pie and try to calm the dog. It's your only hope of stopping it from attacking you. Go to 125

(46) **Growls and Snarls** Go to 114

(47) **A Loud Noise** Go to 122

(48) **A Young Child** Befriend the girl and gain her confidence. She will surely be able to help you find the lord's chamber. Go to 101

(49) **A Riddle** Your name. It is precious to you, other people say it more than you do, you are never without it, and it doesn't weigh a thing! Go to 7

(50) **A Game** Go to 126

(51) **The Lord's Chamber** Whisper to the girl to hide with you in the secret room. Otherwise, she might give the game away to the woman who's calling her name. Go to 93

(52) **Hide-and-Seek** Go to 48

(53) **A Locked Trapdoor** Go to 84

(54) **Mystery Key** Go to 88

(55) **Glinting Gems** Take the ring. Unlike the sword and crown, it is light enough to carry easily – and it will make a valuable gift for your mother. Go to 80

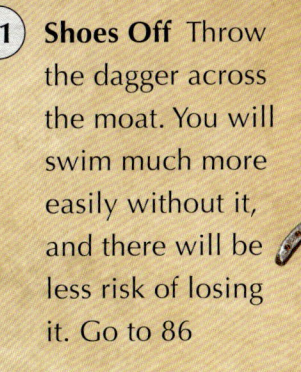

(56) **Sparkling Gift** Go to 21

(57) **A Way Out?** Keep going and feel your way down the steps. People are looking for you and there's no time to lose. Go to 5

(58) **Danger!** Go to 70

(59) **Trapped!** Keep trying to push at the grille. There's no point in going back inside the castle now! Go to 120

(60) **Out!** Go to 105

(61) **Shoes Off** Throw the dagger across the moat. You will swim much more easily without it, and there will be less risk of losing it. Go to 86

(62) **A Mighty Throw** Go to 14

(63) **Wolf!** Yes, you must risk swimming across the moat. It's your only chance of escape and wolves hardly ever attack people. Go to 40

(64) **The Other Side** Go to 56

(65) **Secret Signal** You've escaped the medieval castle!

THE HERALDIC WHEEL

The heraldic wheel on the front cover shows important medieval symbols. Each one will help you find your way through the castle. Discover what the symbols mean below.

- The portcullis is a symbol of protection.
- The raven represents wisdom.
- Water signifies difficult encounters.
- The throne is the symbol of a ruler.
- The fleur de lis represents purity.
- The castle is the symbol of safety.
- The horse represents intelligence.
- The bear signifies great strength.
- The knight represents honour and duty.
- The helmet represents protection.
- Stars signify honour and fortune.
- The unicorn is a symbol of virtue.
- The lion is a symbol of bravery.
- Crossed axes symbolise authority.
- Crossed swords represent freedom and strength.
- The three keys unlock knowledge.
- The rose is a symbol of hope and beauty.
- The dragon is a valiant guardian.
- The crown is the emblem of power.
- The dog is a sign of loyalty and courage.
- The eagle is a symbol of freedom.